ROUGH WATERS AHEAD

MIDDLE SCHOOL TALKS

FAITH SEIGLIE

TRILOGY
A WHOLLY OWNED SUBSIDIARY OF TBN
PROFESSIONAL PUBLISHING MEETS POWERFUL PROMOTION

Trilogy Christian Publishers
A Wholly Owned Subsidiary of Trinity Broadcasting Network
2442 Michelle Drive
Tustin, CA 92780

Copyright © 2024 by Faith Seiglie

All Scripture quotations, unless otherwise noted, are taken from the Holy Bible, New Living Translation, copyright © 1996, 2004, 2015 by Tyndale House Foundation. Used by permission of Tyndale House Publishers, Inc., Carol Stream, Illinois 60188. All rights reserved.

Scripture quotations marked ESV are taken from the ESV® Bible (The Holy Bible, English Standard Version®), copyright © 2001 by Crossway Bibles, a publishing ministry of Good News Publishers. Used by permission. All rights reserved.

Scripture quotations marked NIV are taken from the Holy Bible, New International Version®, NIV®. Copyright © 1973, 1978, 1984, 2011 by Biblica, Inc.TM Used by permission of Zondervan. All rights reserved worldwide. www.zondervan.com. The "NIV" and "New International Version" are trademarks registered in the United States Patent and Trademark Office by Biblica, Inc.TM

Scripture quotations marked NKJV are taken from the New King James Version®. Copyright © 1982 by Thomas Nelson. Used by permission. All rights reserved.

Scripture quotations marked (KJV) are taken from The Holy Bible, King James Version. Cambridge Edition: 1769.

All rights reserved, including the right to reproduce this book or portions thereof in any form whatsoever.

For information, address Trilogy Christian Publishing
Rights Department, 2442 Michelle Drive, Tustin, CA 92780.

Trilogy Christian Publishing/ TBN and colophon are trademarks of Trinity Broadcasting Network.

For information about special discounts for bulk purchases, please contact Trilogy Christian Publishing.

Trilogy Disclaimer: The views and content expressed in this book are those of the author and may not necessarily reflect the views and doctrine of Trilogy Christian Publishing or the Trinity Broadcasting Network.

10 9 8 7 6 5 4 3 2 1
Library of Congress Cataloging-in-Publication Data is available.
ISBN 979-8-89597-116-1
ISBN 979-8-89597-117-8

TABLE OF CONTENTS

Preface: From My Heart to Yours.................... 7

Chapter 1: Drama, Drama, Drama!
           Its Origin and How to Handle It........... 11

Chapter 2: Sticks and Stones
           Social Acceptance and Your Moral
           Compass............................... 23

Chapter 3: My Brain Made Me Do It................ 33

Chapter 4: What's in a Name?
           Figuring Out My Sexuality 43

Chapter 5: Your Epidermis Is Showing
           Insecurities vs. God's Love.............. 53

An Afterword about Your Soul..................... 65

About the Author................................ 67

PREFACE
FROM MY HEART TO YOURS

Let's be honest, this is the page that most people skip. As you can imagine, now that it's my turn to write a preface to a book, I totally get why they are so important…you get to hear the motivation and heart of the author.

Allow me to take you back to 1969. I was just an elementary-aged kid. My best friend was my same age. One summer we decided to play school and recruit a couple of neighborhood prekindergartners as our students. We taught them to read simple consonant-vowel-consonant words and to solve simple math equations. We never doubted our ability to teach or our "students'" ability to learn. From that summer until now, I still hold the same expectations. Yes, I admit it, I'm a born teacher. Oh, I tried other areas of study in college, but once I took that first "Introduction to Education" course, it was like a well-worn glove fitting over my hand.

My start was in the elementary grade levels, but

my passion was found in a classroom full of middle schoolers. I loved them! No two days were the same, as each brought new behaviors, drama, and challenges for more than a decade of my teaching career. As a follower of Christ teaching in public schools, I understood the expectations of the school boards. A Bible was visible on my desk, and when appropriate, Biblical wisdom was quoted without references, yet my students knew I was a Christian. Therefore, my students who were also Christians sought conversation and advice from me. Often, I knew the parents of these students, so I felt free to share from God's Word. However, our brief conversations were often forgotten, and I often hoped to place something more concrete in their hands. I found plenty of Christian reading material for younger children and older teens, but very little geared toward the age where changes happen the most—middle school. It's my opinion that these crucial three years are the most vital to be reached with the Gospel of Christ. As humans, we go through the most rapid physical changes of our lives during puberty. Therefore, it stands to reason that other areas of humanness can, and probably do, as well. We come into the age of accountability.

So out of this mindset, the book you now hold was

born. Because each chapter ends with brief journaling, perhaps this book could be used in a youth or small group setting. I'm not sure how God will use it. What I do know is that He put on my heart a desire to encourage middle-aged adolescents. To let them know that they are not alone in their struggles and to reassure them of the love of their Creator, our Father and the God of the Universe. "For as high as the heavens are above the earth, so great is his steadfast love toward those who fear him" (Psalm 103:11, ESV).

CHAPTER 1

DRAMA, DRAMA, DRAMA! ITS ORIGIN AND HOW TO HANDLE IT

What comes to your mind when you hear the word "drama"? It's probably not the definition in Webster's dictionary nor the one your language arts teacher has taught you. Yet you know exactly what it means in the context of social media, within friend groups, and at the school lunch table. In real life it means conflict! Anyone living between the ages of…well, just living, has or will have a brush with drama sooner or later. Some people like to start it, others like to fuel it, some curiously observe, and others do everything in their power to avoid it! Doesn't matter which group you think describes you, eventually drama will find you. Why? It's a pretty simple answer: we are human.

You've probably already figured out that humans aren't perfect. Included in that long list of imperfections, we find insecurities. It's these insecurities that can drive us to put others down to lift ourselves—that's the kind of drama I'm talking about here. It's the one that's most common in middle school. Think about the last time you heard gossip about someone. Did it lift them up or put them down? Think about the last time you saw someone treated unfairly at school or while hanging out with a group of friends. Who walked away feeling more powerful? At that moment, the person who verbalized the witty put-downs gained the admiration of the status quo, but this satisfaction is brief. I often felt concern for my students who habitually felt the need to put others down to make themselves look better. It was a sign they were dealing with insecurities that were most likely the result of deep-down hurt. You see, some emotional hurts can be so deep that the pressure to verbally or physically hurt others (or themselves) is the natural response. But there's a cure for those hurts and insecurities; it's giving those hurts to Someone who loves you unconditionally.

ORIGIN OF DRAMA

Way back at the beginning of time, I mean the very beginning, drama didn't exist. We find this drama-free existence in the second chapter of Genesis, the first book of the Bible. It's a beautiful account of how

DRAMA, DRAMA, DRAMA!

God made a companion, later named Eve, just for Adam! He was so happy to have another creation like him! They were perfect for each other, quite literally! However, with the very first verse of Genesis 3 we see trouble coming. Have you ever noticed how life's drama is usually based on a mix of half-truths or half-lies? Same difference, right? After all, if drama were based on truth alone or bold-faced lies, it wouldn't be nearly as interesting!

Genesis 3 starts with the biggest half-truth ever told, and mankind hasn't been the same since. God had told Adam back in Genesis 2 that he could eat the fruit from any tree that he wanted except for one, and that one tree was the knowledge of good and evil. Do you know the difference between good and evil? Well then, you already know how this story ends, but here's how it went down in Genesis 3:1–13 (all Bible verses are from the New Living Translation unless otherwise noted):

> *The serpent was the shrewdest of all the wild animals the LORD God had made. One day he asked the woman, "Did God really say you must not eat the fruit from any of the trees in the garden?"*

ROUGH WATERS AHEAD

Okay, pause here. Why wasn't Eve shocked by the talking snake? Could some animals talk before this ultimate drama went down? There are many people far smarter than me that have some thoughts about this. But the bottom line is that the devil was doing the talking through the serpent. See Revelation 12:9 and Revelation 20:2 for more clarification. Let's get back to Genesis 3:

> *"Of course we may eat fruit from the trees in the garden," the woman replied. "It's only the fruit of the tree in the middle of the garden that we are not allowed to eat. God said, 'You must not eat it or even touch it; if you do, you will die.'"*
>
> *"You won't die!" the serpent replied to the woman. "God knows that your eyes will be opened as soon as you eat it, and you will be like God, knowing both good and evil."*
>
> *The woman was convinced. She saw that the tree was beautiful and its fruit looked delicious, and she wanted the wisdom it would give her. Then she gave some to her husband, who was with her, and he ate it, too. At that moment their eyes were*

> *opened, and they suddenly felt shame at their nakedness. So they sewed fig leaves together to cover themselves.*

Did you catch the half-truth? Adam and Eve suddenly saw their nakedness and tried to cover themselves. Why would they do this if they didn't have a revelation of good and evil? That part of what the serpent told them was true. Are Adam and Eve still walking around today? But the serpent said they wouldn't die. That was the lie. Even though they didn't die right after eating the fruit, their disobedience in eating the fruit that God had told them not to eat started the dying process, kind of like starting a timer—it's called aging! Sadly for mankind, two deaths occurred that day—physical and spiritual. We are sorrowfully familiar with physical death, but did you know the spirit part of us died, too? That's why Jesus said, "You must be born again" in John 3:7.

So how did God respond to all of this drama? Let's keep reading from Genesis 3.

> *When the cool evening breezes were blowing, the man and his wife heard the LORD God walking about in the garden. So they hid from the LORD God among the trees. Then the LORD God called to*

ROUGH WATERS AHEAD

the man, "Where are you?"

He replied, "I heard you walking in the garden, so I hid. I was afraid because I was naked."

"Who told you that you were naked?" the LORD God asked. "Have you eaten from the tree whose fruit I commanded you not to eat?"

The man replied, "It was the woman you gave me who gave me the fruit, and I ate it."

Then the LORD God asked the woman, "What have you done?"

"The serpent deceived me," she replied. "That's why I ate it." (This is the first recorded game of blame in history!)

Next, God issues the consequences for each participant in this first very real drama. Those consequences are still seen today. Men have to work for a living, childbirth is painful for women, and snakes slither around on their bellies; and yes, we will all die—eventually. However, God gave hope at this lowest moment. He prophesied the coming of Jesus Christ, the Messiah, and even killed an animal to use its skin to clothe Adam and his wife. This exemplified how Jesus Christ would one day die to cover our sins. You can read for yourself in Genesis 3:14–24.

You might be asking, "Why did God let this happen? Why did He put the tree of knowledge of good and evil in the garden in the first place?" From the very first words of, "Let there be light," this was, and still is, all part of God's loving plan. You see, God didn't want little robot creatures. This whole drama played out in this way because God values your free choice. In fact, He values your free choice so much that He will allow you to choose hell over His saving love. Yes, it's your choice. It's absolutely true that God is love, and He proved it by sending His only Son, Jesus Christ, to die on the Cross as payment for your sin.

God knew all along during the six days of creation that it would cost Him seeing His most beloved Son suffer under the weight of everyone's sin and die to be the only pure and acceptable sacrifice to put humans back in right standing with Him. Jesus Christ then rose again three days later, as prophesied, to punctuate that what the devil meant for evil, He wills to be good! All you have to do is ask Jesus to forgive you and receive Him into your heart. "But if we confess our sins to him, he is faithful and just to forgive us our sins and to cleanse us from all wickedness. (1 John 1:9). It's a choice either to remain in your sinful state or to receive the rescue of God's love.

TO BE OR NOT TO BE... DRAWN INTO DRAMA

So in getting back to drama in today's world, how can you keep yourself from starting or being drawn into our human tendency towards drama? Realize the place from where it's coming. Did you have a hand in whatever drama is circulating, possibly bringing the consequences on yourself? If you have had a part in some drama, tell the truth and apologize. This isn't easy and certainly not popular. Also, refrain from playing the blame game, or else it's Adam, Eve, and the serpent all over again! Be brave and do the right thing. I can't promise it will improve the situation, but it will improve your conscience.

Now let's flip the drama coin over and look at the other side. Are you honestly shocked to hear an untrue rumor about yourself or someone you care about? It's realistic that there are certain circumstances in which you might have to advocate for yourself by stating what's true and using your words to stop the action. You might even need help from a trusted adult if the situation is persistent or unsafe.

DRAMA, DRAMA, DRAMA!

However, if you're blindsided by a nasty rumor, you probably know firsthand that our first reaction is to get defensive and retaliate. Instead of getting defensive, try going on the offensive. Have you ever seen a wrestling match? I don't know much about this sport, but as an observer it can look like one opponent is about to win when, wham! One unexpected but carefully calculated move on the mat flips the script (and the opponent)! Well, this two-word action will flip the script in much the same way when it comes to most drama. This two-word action is…wait for it…walk away! You might need to walk away emotionally, mentally, physically, or all three! This takes a massive amount of self-control, but just know in the end that you didn't give away your power. Let me explain…. Did you know there's an invisible transfer of personal power when you allow someone to push your proverbial buttons? In the heat of drama and conflict, don't give away your power! Choose to walk away!

WRAP-UP

If you're being impacted by drama right now at school, home, neighborhood, or on social media, ask yourself this reflective question: are you being part of the solution or part of the problem? If you're being part of the problem, the good news is that you can change sides! Simply decide to be part of the solution. How? The best solutions come from God's Word. "A gentle answer deflects anger, but harsh words make tempers flare" (Proverbs 15:1). Apply the advice the apostle Paul wrote to young Timothy, "...run from all these evil things" (1 Timothy 6:11). Tell God you need His help. First Corinthians 10:13 in the English Standard Version says that God will "provide a way of escape." So, the next time you get tempted to start drama or sense that drama is brewing, don't engage! Instead, look for the escape route!

DRAMA, DRAMA, DRAMA!

REFLECT AND WRITE

Think about the last time you were in conflict with someone like a friend, sibling, parent, or teacher. Did you choose to be part of the problem or part of the solution? If the solution, write about what you did. (You probably want to share this shining moment if you're in a group setting.)

However, if you were part of the problem, write about it and decide how to be part of the solution if it happens again. (You might not be so eager to share this tidbit, but that's okay. You've got a game plan moving forward now!)

_____
_____
_____
_____
_____
_____
_____
_____

ROUGH WATERS AHEAD

CHAPTER 2

STICKS AND STONES SOCIAL ACCEPTANCE AND YOUR MORAL COMPASS

Perhaps one of the biggest changes you will see in your friends, peers, or even in yourself as you trek through your teen years is social awareness and the subsequent need for social acceptance. This need to be accepted by our peers is in our DNA. You might begin to care more about your choice of clothing, hairstyle, or anything right down to your school supplies. Of all the issues that I saw my students struggle with most, the effort for social acceptance was at the top of the list. Our desire to fit into a social group at school, church, or extracurricular activity is natural. After all, the fear of being made fun of or rejected by our peers is very real.

Social awareness can actually be a good thing. Let's be honest, we're all thankful for this social awareness when our peers apply deodorant after gym class! Some kids, however, can be aware that they stink but do not care to do anything about it. But if given enough negative social cues (nobody wants to sit next to them for the rest of the day), those kids will eventually want to be socially accepted and toss some deo in their gym bag. In this way, social pressure benefits the community (those in the class after gym).

But for some teens the awareness and need for social acceptance is more keenly felt and can cause them to compromise their values or even become a different person, depending on who they're hanging out with. This is called social desirability bias. Let's bring in an example here. Imagine that you join a sports team. As the practices go on, certain team members continually put down a teammate and call it joking around. You might find yourself laughing at a comment that you really don't agree with, just so you'll fit in. This is social desirability bias in action. It's okay to want social acceptance, but at what cost?

SOCIAL ACCEPTANCE

Social acceptance is the desire to be accepted, included, and respected by a social group. Social acceptance can be a strong influence on our behavior choices, and this influence can either result in a positive or negative outcome.

Let's look at an example of a positive outcome of social acceptance. Each year on the National Day of Prayer, students met at our school's flagpole before school began. As small handfuls of students were exiting homerooms and leaving the hallways to attend, their curious peers would ask where they were going. A few of these peers would join their ranks, then a few more, until the crowd grew to a sizable group of kids leaving the building! Even though most students had no forethought of participating in the event that morning, they made a positive behavior choice because it was a social event that welcomed everyone, and they felt socially accepted in that group. (And yes, it got them out of class for a few minutes.)

In contrast, almost every school year some of my top students were caught aiding and abetting fellow classmates by sharing answers to tests, class and homework assignments. When these students were asked what motivated this lapse in both character and judgment, the answer basically boiled down to the need for social acceptance. The desire to be socially accepted can be a powerful influence on behavior choices, and in negative circumstances it can cause very real moral dilemmas for middle schoolers. Just remember that behavior choices that feel wrong probably are. That's your conscience talking, and it means you actually have one, which is a very good thing! Realize that the need for social acceptance can test your beliefs about what is morally right or wrong and even your beliefs about God. This is why you need to develop a strong moral compass!

SO WHAT'S A MORAL COMPASS?

You've probably learned about the compass rose. It's that symbol on a map that shows the cardinal directions, like north, south, east, and west. Your moral compass is very similar. It's what you call right, wrong, or somewhere in between. Just as you use a compass rose to find direction on a map, your moral compass gives direction for your life—your whole life!

The difference is that a compass rose on a map will always indicate true north, while your moral compass is developed by your power of reasoning right and wrong. Everyone has a basic moral compass—it's called a conscience. Remember what happened at the tree of the knowledge of good and evil? Not only do we know good from evil, but because we are born into sin, you can probably guess that the bent of our natural human reasoning is tainted. That's why humans can reason good to be bad and bad to be good. We can choose to let the fallen world system, which belongs to Satan, develop our moral compass, or we can place our moral compass on the map of God's Word, the Bible. It's our true north!

By this time in your life, you probably have made your mind up about such moral issues as lying, cheating, and dishonesty. You might still have times when you occasionally give in to temptation to lie, cheat, or steal, but if asked, you would say these are morally wrong. Your moral compass has been set regarding these morals. However, have you pondered weightier morals like alcohol, drugs, gender questioning, homosexuality, and premarital sex? Being intentional about knowing what God has to say about these heavy issues will most definitely set your moral compass in the right direction. It can safeguard you from having lifelong regrets. Additionally, it's the secret weapon for sudden temptations that are going down in real time!

Knowing what God's Word says about morals, ethics, and values creates a strong moral compass and helps you to know who you are on the inside, the person God created you to be. This is empowering! When others try to tempt you, make fun of you when standing your ground, pull you into their drama, or just push your buttons, consult your moral compass! Know that you are God's child, the righteousness of God in Christ Jesus! (See 2 Cor. 5:21.) Your power is who you are on the inside, knowing that you are a loved child of God Almighty!

GOD'S MANUAL FOR OUR MORAL COMPASS

Developing your moral compass takes time, so don't give up if you blow it and do something that goes completely south. We slip, stumble, and maybe even fall. (I sure have, multiple times.) We live in a body that is called flesh in the Bible. Remember the spirit man who is now alive if you are born again? Well, the spirit wars against the flesh and vice versa. (See Galatians 5:17.) But there's hope! Jesus inside of us is greater than all the schemes of the devil and his fleshly temptations. We might fall down, but we don't have to stay there! (See 1 John 4:4.)

To get your moral compass pointing in the right direction, let's look at a few words from God's Manual for Life, aka the Bible. Proverbs 12:22 reads, "The LORD detests lying lips, but he delights in those who tell the truth." Leviticus 19:11 warns, "Do not steal. Do not deceive or cheat one another." Psalm 37:4 says, "Take delight in the LORD, and he will give you your

STICKS AND STONES

heart's desires." Philippians 4:8 exhorts, "Fix your thoughts on what is true, and honorable, and right, and pure, and lovely, and admirable. Think about things that are excellent and worthy of praise." Wow, that's quite challenging, but not impossible!

Unlike the lie that the devil wants you to believe, God's Word is not a list of do's and don'ts. It's actually filled with messages of love and encouragement! If you have bought a new video game or gadget, it probably came with some type of manual or website for troubleshooting. It probably wasn't even necessary to read this manual to start using this game or gadget. However, if you run into a problem, probably the first thing you'll do is troubleshoot using the manual that the inventor or designer wrote for such instances. In the same way, God created mankind and He wrote a manual for us! It's God's Word, the Bible.

WRAP-UP

God knows life is hard because of the world's fallen state, and our choices can make it even harder! Because He loves and wants the best for us, He has given us the Bible filled with instructions and parameters. Think of it like this: You see a friend playing in a busy street. Most likely, drivers will see your friend and swerve around or honk the horn. Your friend might be fine playing in the busy street for a while, but you know the chances are very high that something bad will eventually happen. So in your loving concern, you will go out and warn your friend. So it is with our loving heavenly Father. God created us; He knows how we are flawed, and He knows that playing in the street (aka the world) will eventually be disastrous! Choosing God's Word as our moral compass not only keeps us from making regrettable mistakes but will offer troubleshooting advice when we do mess up.

STICKS AND STONES

REFLECT AND WRITE

If your moral compass chooses to stand for the right thing, you might risk being the only one left standing. I like to call these situations character-building moments, and they are not for the faint of heart. The good thing about these moments is that they are short-lived, yet filled with lifelong satisfaction. If there's one catch phrase that my students heard me say often, it's this: Good decisions bring good things (eventually) and bad decisions bring bad things (also eventually), and life, for the most part, is that simple!

Think of a time when your moral compass helped you make a good decision. Now write it below and share it with someone.

_____

_____

_____

_____

_____

_____

_____

ROUGH WATERS AHEAD

CHAPTER 3
MY BRAIN MADE ME DO IT

Sometimes good kids will do bad things, and sometimes bad kids will do good things. It's true! I've sat in parent-teacher conferences where a parent just can't believe their sweet little snookums cheated on a test! Sure, it was out of character for that particular student to cheat, but for whatever reason, it happened. On the other hand, I've witnessed the meanest bully in the class pick a dropped pencil off the floor and return it to the owner. (Yes, I've also seen them gleefully snap it in two pieces!) My point is that enigmas happen!

Middle schoolers can be puzzling. Maybe that's why I loved teaching them so much—no two days of school were ever the same! If there's ever a time when you are tempted to try new behaviors, it's in middle school. Blame your prefrontal cortex for this! Along with all the hormonal changes that are giving you acne and body odor, your brain is also experiencing some changes. Located near the front of your head, actually behind your forehead, the prefrontal cortex is busily redeveloping your ability to reason. It's the kind of reasoning that prioritizes (i.e., I should study for that science test instead of playing video games) and makes decisions (i.e., I should just return this pencil to the owner).

WHAT'S IN A BRAIN?

Because your prefrontal cortex is doing a remodeling job during adolescence, you might have some difficulty deciding to do the right or wrong thing, especially in real time. Remember the moral compass? Having given some predetermined thought to your values will be helpful in these moments. However, understanding your brain development during your adolescent years could provide some clarity as to why making good choices can be so easy and so elusive at the same time.

To kick off our "brain discussion," let me ask you when you stopped believing fictional characters were real, like the tooth fairy. It's one of the questions I loved asking my middle school students. Almost always, the answer was around their seventh or eighth birthday. Why? Your brain has experienced quite a bit of physical growth by the age of six. In fact, it's nearly its adult size. Then something else happens during ages six to eight—you become less gullible. Try telling a three-year-old that milk comes from the cow that lives in your fridge and compare that response with one from an eight-year-old.

Your initial reasoning and emotional responses are developed by your early childhood experiences, and with each new experience, your brain created pathways and connections. Now as you move closer to age eleven, your brain does something amazing. You know how a phone or computer needs updating? Well, the same thing begins to happen to the preteen brain!

To begin explaining this process, you need to know that your brain is a collection of tightly packed human tissue called gray matter. Within your gray matter are many types of specific cells and blood capillaries. One specific cell is the nerve cell. This cell looks a little like a root bulb (nucleus) with tiny root-like projections coming out called axons and dendrites. Nerve impulses, aka electrochemical impulses, travel from nerve cell to nerve cell along these pathways formed by the axons and dendrites. (Pausing here to say that this rudimentary lesson on the brain will have to do for now, but it's way more complex than this!)

As you encountered new information in your early years, these axons and dendrites formed pathways for nerve impulses to travel throughout your brain. Then during adolescence, any pathways in your brain that are no longer needed or being used are pruned back, like the pruning that might be done to a rosebush. Why? To strengthen highly used pathways that will give your brain a power boost for your adult years. You've heard the quip "use it or lose" it, right? That's what this pruning process is all about.

Now for the zinger…this pruning process begins at the back of your brain, meaning that your prefrontal cortex (the place for reasoning) is last to be updated! To top it off, this process can last well into your mid-twenties! Once this process is mostly completed, your power to reason and make better decisions should override the tendencies for risky behaviors or emotional decisions. (Now you know why there's a legal age limit to consuming alcoholic beverages. Take a teen brain that's still being updated and add alcohol—well, that could equal a staggering teen death statistic!)

BEWARE OF THE AMYGDALA

Have you ever noticed how mature you can be in one situation and in another completely revert back to the behavior of a five-year-old? This is proof that your brain is still in the process of being pruned, meaning your shining moment of maturity most likely came from that part of the brain that's been recently updated, and the thumb-sucking meltdown or risky behavior probably came from the part of the brain that's still in the queue for the update! Until the pruning process is complete, the part of the brain called the amygdala is in charge of reasoning, a left-over of your childhood brain. You should know that this part of the brain is associated with more instinctive behavior, like emotions and impulses. To add insult to injury, throw in physical and hormonal changes and it's no wonder growing up is tough!

As an illustration of the adolescent brain, I recall a school morning when two of my eighth-grade girls barreled into homeroom period in sheer panic mode! They were stepsisters and shared a bedroom in their ground-level house. Earlier that morning their boyfriends thought it would be daring to drop by the girls' house on their way to school and peck on their bedroom window. The girls, being equally daring, invited the boys to crawl in through the window. It wasn't long before the muffled and deeper male voices of the boyfriends were heard through the door by the father of the house. Before they knew it, the father of the house was pounding on the locked door, causing the boyfriends to flee for their lives out the same window!

That's not the worst of it though. The girls didn't want to get in trouble, so they lied and told their father that these were random men who had just broken into their bedroom through the window. Immediately, the father grabbed his rifle and was in hot pursuit! The sisters didn't know what to do, so they stuck with the routine and got on the school bus. Now they were frantically relaying this story to me, afraid for the lives of their boyfriends! Talk about the amygdala part of the brain being in full control! Immediately, they were instructed to call their dad to tell the truth! Two lives depended on it! Obviously, the pruning process hadn't reached the prefrontal cortex of all brains involved in this fiasco!

Let's use this illustration to segue to another important topic that impacts the moral compass. When is it right to "tell on" someone? Many middle schoolers see this as "narking," and it is often considered the ultimate bane or ruination of their reputation. So here's the rule of thumb: If what you know is going to hurt you, hurt someone else, or hurt someone's property, you need to tell a trusted adult. Period.

BRAINS UNDER CONSTRUCTION

If you've been told how mature you are by your family members or teachers, it might be difficult to keep living up to their expectations. It feels good on the inside to know you're growing up, but don't be too hard on yourself if you let yourself or others down. Your brain is under construction! This also goes for your peers whose brains might be on a slower pruning schedule than yours or others your age. So, don't be persuaded to do something against your better judgment by a brain that's less pruned than yours!

Because your brain is under construction into your twenties, it's probably a good idea to pump the brakes when it comes to making decisions about issues that you will be dealing with in your adult years. Okay, let's get specific. Think about the different kinds of decisions that average kids your age make in the flow of a day. It's probably things like what to wear, what to eat, what friends to hang with, or what activities are planned for that day. These are probably basic decisions for kids your age. Most likely you're not deciding which job opportunity to take, whether or not to buy a house, or choosing who you're going to marry (although you might be wishing). Better decisions on these issues will be made if you wait to let your brain fully update!

WRAP-UP

It's a real temptation for teens to think they're mature enough to handle "adult" situations. This kind of thinking forces them to make decisions their brains might not be ready to make. Maybe you know someone your age who attended a party hosted by an older sibling or friend where drinking and smoking (or worse) were present. Most likely they survived it and maybe even laughed about it later; however, if they made some wrong choices at the party, these choices changed them. Their brains just weren't updated enough to see the troubled waters of the consequences ahead. A little bit of their innocence was sacrificed in the name of growing up. Regret always, always, always follows wrong choices.

We saw the same reaction from Adam and Eve after eating from the tree of knowledge of good and evil. Satan hasn't changed his tactics on mankind for thousands of years; he just repeats the same lies on the next generation. But with a fully updated brain AND renewed mind, you will overcome any temptation. Romans 12:2 gives us some great advice on minimizing our regrets: "Don't copy the behavior and customs of this world, but let God transform you into a new person by changing the way you think. Then you will learn to know God's will for you, which is good and pleasing and perfect."

REFLECT AND WRITE

Scenario: You are spending the night with a friend. Your friend receives a text message from another friend that you don't know very well, inviting you both to a party just a few houses down. Your friend wants to sneak out to go, but you don't know the person who is texting very well or if their parents are home. You don't know who else is invited or their ages. Plus, sneaking out isn't a good idea either. So far, you have a trusting relationship with your parents. Of course, your moral compass is telling you this isn't a good idea. But your prefrontal cortex is busily reasoning out the pros and cons. Plus, you don't want your parents to think badly about your friend or get them in trouble. Is there a way of escape? What will you do?

_____

_____

_____

ROUGH WATERS AHEAD

CHAPTER 4

WHAT'S IN A NAME?
FIGURING OUT MY SEXUALITY

Innocence is a good thing. In the days of Creation before man's disobedience, God called everything that He made good. Adam and Eve lived together in the Garden of Eden in complete nakedness as proof of their innocence, and it was good! It didn't last, however, and due to their disobedience, humans now have a fallen nature that can be as corrupt and perverse as can be imagined.

Because the discussion of sexual orientation in our culture keeps spiraling down to younger and younger children, robbing them of their innocence, we can't tiptoe around this topic waiting until they're "old enough." If you attend school (particularly a public one), hang with neighborhood friends, listen to music, play video games, or stream on a device, you've probably seen or heard some words related to sexual orientation like transgender, bisexual, binary, homosexuality, or lesbian. You might have witnessed these forms of sexuality within your family or friends. Maybe you've been pondering questions about your own sexual orientation. You are not alone in your thoughts. We're all human, and every human has had these thoughts—even thousands of years ago!

POP CULTURE AND SEX

Popular culture is the devil's domain. In John 16:11 (KJV), Jesus calls him the "prince of this world." Without knowing what God's Word says about sex and having His Holy Spirit living inside of us, popular culture will influence our thoughts on the matter of sexuality.

So what does God's Word say about sex? The Bible actually has quite a bit to say on the subject, but I'm just giving a few verses here. Genesis 1:27 says, "So God created human beings in his own image. In the image of God he created them; male and female he created them." Genesis 2:24 (NIV) reads, "That is why a man leaves his father and mother and is united to his wife, and they become one flesh." Hebrews 13:4a exhorts, "Give honor to marriage, and remain faithful to one another in marriage."

WHAT'S IN A NAME? FIGURING OUT MY SEXUALITY

Although it's popular in today's culture to accept alternative lifestyles, God says otherwise in His Word. Leviticus 18:22 reads, "Do not practice homosexuality, having sex with another man as with a woman. It is a detestable sin." Wow! That verse alone hits alternative lifestyles right between the eyes! Check out Romans 1:26–27 and 1 Corinthians 6:9–10 to know more about what God's Word says about this topic. To sum it up, however, I think it's safe to say that God's Word is clear and simple when it comes to sex. He intends it to be a beautiful act between a man and a woman who are married, end of discussion. After all, He wrote the "manual" (aka the Bible) for us to get the best out of this life.

However, when God created mankind, one of His most important must-haves on His list for you and me was free will. Do you know what other spiritual creature knows you have free will? Remember the lie that the devil told Adam and Eve about eating from the tree of the knowledge of good and evil? Lies and deception are at the top of the devil's human trickery list, and he's been spewing the same lies over generations for thousands of years, particularly when it comes to sex! King Solomon puts it best in Ecclesiastes 1:9 (NIV), "What has been will be again, what has been done will be done again; there is nothing new under the sun." Our current culture on various sexual orientations might seem like new ideas, but now you know that's not true. Even without the Bible, archeologists have uncovered the existence of sexual perverseness in ancient cultures.

Maybe you've been told some of the devil's lies that it's natural curiosity to look at sexual body parts and actions online. Maybe you've heard that sex before marriage is okay if the parties involved have given their consent. You may have even read that same-sex attraction is just another option. Have any of these ideas ever passed through your thoughts? Because we live in a body and have a mind, did you know that the devil can gain access into our lives through the free will of our thoughts? Our mind is a powerful portal into our souls! Actually, your mind is the battleground between your fleshly (worldly) man and your born-again spirit man. If spirit man hasn't been born again, then worldly thoughts seem right every time!

On the other hand, the born again spirit man gives your mind a fighting chance! Apply God's Word to your thoughts and you will see right through the devil's lies. In Genesis 1:27 God clearly gave us His thoughts on gender confusion: "So God created human beings in his own image. In the image of God he created them; male and female he created them." The book of Psalms declares, "You made all the delicate, inner parts of my body and knit me together in my mother's womb" (Psalm 139:13). So if the enemy of your soul has dropped thoughts into your mind about your sexual identity that don't line up with God's Word, and you are born again, recognize where those thoughts came from and send them packing in the name of Jesus Christ!

Remember what we learned in the last chapter about the human brain and how it isn't able to reason fully during adolescence? So let's bring that fact into context here. Can a teenage brain determine that they are ready for sex or a sex change? Are their brains ready to reason out and deal with the long-term consequences of these choices when they become adults? These questions are definitely worth the effort to ponder. In the current culture that promotes gender confusion as young as pre-school, this one point is completely true and clear from God's Word: God made you either male or female, brain and all. To think or say anything different than this is to tell God that He made a mistake when He made you. Do you really think that the God of the universe would make that kind of mistake? Not at all! God knew you before time began. God's Word says that He has and is always thinking about you! Don't believe the lie that you are anything different than how you were knit together in your mother's womb!

TECHNOLOGY'S IMPACT ON SEX

Let's push out even further to look at the bigger picture. Are you seeing a worldwide advance of the devil to introduce younger and younger children to sexual alternatives? Even educational television shows geared toward preschoolers display alternative family units. It's no secret that the advancement of technology has made sexual perversion so easily accessible to children and teens. They are able to view things on the internet that their brains just aren't ready to process. This robs them of their innocence and plants seeds of images that can mess with their minds. Just like back in the Garden of Eden, the serpent's suggestion to eat the forbidden fruit seemed intriguing and even right, but it brought death into our world. Sexual temptations are just like that delicious-looking fruit that Eve pondered eating. Sexual temptations, too, will bring death—death to innocence, death to integrity, and even death to future relationships.

However, we now know God's Word on the subject and that His ways for us are best! Why are His ways best? Because God loves you the most! More than your parents, your grandparents, or your girlfriend or boyfriend. First Corinthians 6:20 says, "For God bought you with a high price. So you must honor God with your body." Now think about the apps and tabs saved on your electronic devices. You might need to go home and delete a few things off your phone or tablet. Be assured that God's love is there to forgive and restore.

WRAP-UP

It's true that God created us as sexual beings, but He also gave instructions to get the most out of it without shame. Sitting by a warm fire roasting marshmallows on a cool night brings satisfaction; however, a raging forest fire brings devastation. Fire within the boundaries of a fire pit is good, while fire allowed to run wild burns everything in its path. The same is true for sex! In talking with my students over the years, lots of teens want to know where the boundaries are when it comes to physical contact between boys and girls. It's actually an easy answer: If you can do it (whatever "it" is), say it, see it, wear it, or hear it with Jesus Christ by your side, then it's okay. This is an easy-to-remember, life-time, foolproof, guilt-free moral standard. I can personally attest, it works!

In my line of work, I've seen one too many students deal with the regret and shame of choosing to become sexually active too early in life. Your virginity is a gift that you will only give once, so it's a decision that needs to be made with a fully pruned and updated brain that understands why marriage is best. If you've already been sexually active outside of marriage, God can restore and make all things new through true repentance and a change in your mindset. In some situations, it might even take some counseling to break free from the lies that have been masquerading as truth in your mind. I love what Paul writes to the Christians living in Rome: "Do not be conformed to this world but be transformed by the renewal of your mind" (Romans 12:2, ESV). How is our mind renewed? It's so easy—read God's Word and pray! Psalm 119:11 says, "I have stored up your word in my heart, that I might not sin against you." First John 5:3 says, "Loving God means keeping his commandments, and his commandments are not burdensome."

WHAT'S IN A NAME? FIGURING OUT MY SEXUALITY

REFLECT AND WRITE

Suppose you have a friend or family member that chooses an alternative lifestyle. How can you show them the love of Christ, knowing what God's Word says about it?

_____

_____

_____

_____

_____

_____

_____

_____

_____

_____

_____

_____

_____

ROUGH WATERS AHEAD

CHAPTER 5

YOUR EPIDERMIS IS SHOWING INSECURITIES VS. GOD'S LOVE

If you've ever ridden the school bus home, you know firsthand the kind of, dare I say, torture that older riders can impart on younger riders. Though it's difficult to admit a black mark from my past, as an older bus rider my middle school friends and I could throw most any elementary kid into sheer panic by emphatically (and a bit dramatically) warning them that their epidermis was showing. Of course, they had no clue what we were talking about, which increased their anxiety and firmly established our superiority!

This sounds a bit silly now knowing that your epidermis is simply your skin, and everybody's is showing! In contrast, insecurities go a bit deeper than your epidermis. Because of our fallen sin nature, everyone is prone to insecurities. Yes, even the

ROUGH WATERS AHEAD

meanest kid on the bus. Believe it or not, sometimes the meanest person has the deepest insecurities. Have you ever heard that hurting people hurt people? No statement was ever truer! Not to get into your business, but if you disagree with that statement, you probably have a tendency to hurt people and maybe you haven't yet connected the dots.

I once had a student who continually put others down with both her words and actions. She exuded a superior attitude over everyone in the class—over the whole eighth grade, in fact. After many attempts to redirect her words and actions during group work in class, I had to take the situation in hand to protect the learning environment of those in her group. As not to call her out, we wrapped up class that day with one of my mini "character building" talks. Basically, we talked about the motivation behind putting others down, and if you've ever been in the hallways between classes, you know that this is kind of a typical behavior for middle schoolers. Eighth graders are pretty self-aware, so it didn't take much for them to see that put downs are used by people in an attempt to make themselves look better. Immediately after class, this young lady marched up to me and emphatically told me that conclusion was most certainly wrong in her case. Well, at least she had enough self-awareness to know she put others down.

ME? ANXIOUS?

There's probably enough psychological evidence now to prove that insecurities can manifest in many different ways, just one of them being the need to put others down. Insecurities are basically areas in our lives where we don't feel secure. These areas can be physical, like being homeless or without enough food; emotional, like not feeling loved; social, like not being accepted by peers; mental, like feeling you can't cope; or spiritual, like questioning what comes after death. While I'm not trained in counseling or psychology (although I did take a few courses on the subject in college), insecurities seem to exist on a spectrum of sorts and can often produce the feeling of anxiety.

Today, most people would say that they have experienced feeling anxious at some time in their lives, and it appears that anxiety is on the rise in our current culture. What makes this subject even more complex is that on some days people can feel more anxious than on other days. Food, rest, and circumstances all contribute to our anxiety. There are personal "triggers" that can cause anxiety. As you can see, the subject of insecurities and anxiety is very broad and very real! In serious cases, anxiety or insecurities can spiral into depression or self-hatred. These are very dangerous areas to navigate on your own, so I just want to pause here to encourage anyone currently feeling this way to ask for help from a trusted adult. Yes, there's at least one trusted adult someplace in your life, like a parent, youth leader, pastor, school counselor, or teacher. Don't put off talking with a trusted adult, thinking those self-hate feelings will go away on their own. Make a plan to ask for help now.

Have I mentioned that everyone is prone to insecurities? Great, your comprehension is excellent! Let's go back to Chapter 1 to reference the biggest and saddest drama of all, the fall of mankind. This is actually the root of everything negative and evil in our world and lives today, including insecurities.

But do you remember that God didn't walk away, telling Adam and Eve that they blew it, because they did indeed! What did God, our loving Creator, do instead? Genesis 3 reads that He made garments of skin, implying that He first needed to kill an animal to cover their nakedness, which Adam and Eve saw as the result of their disobedience to God. They totally messed up, they deliberately disobeyed God through their own reasoning, they allowed themselves to be deceived by the serpent, and forever changed mankind's standing with a holy and sinless God!

God could no longer commune with them in the cool evenings of the Garden of Eden. Holiness isn't holiness if communed with disobedience, is it? Gratefully, in that moment, God didn't withdraw forever; instead, He provided reconciliation for us! He promised that He would send His only sinless Son to pay for mankind's disobedience. Just as He sacrificed the animal as a covering for Adam and Eve, He sent Jesus Christ, His Son, to be the sacrifice to cover our sins, and His shed blood washes them away forever. Why would God do these things? God is love and He can't help but love us!

In looping back to Genesis 3, we are reminded of the place where all negative human emotions, including insecurity, anxiety, and depression, began. That's the bad news. The good news is that Jesus Christ gave His life so that these negative emotions no longer rule over us if you have been born again. His death broke the power of sin and darkness; see Romans 6:10. There's no denying that we will still have negative emotions from time to time. That's because we still live in a fleshly body. Remember that the Spirit of God in us wars against the flesh that we are? So how does the Spirit of God in us gain the high ground? It's something most Christians struggle with—daily reading God's Word and knowing what it says. Do you know what Psalm 119:11 says? "I have hidden your word in my heart, that I might not sin against you." So there's the answer—read, study, and memorize God's Word.

When I was young, I attended a Christian school that was strong in Bible memorization. I've probably memorized hundreds of verses, but for most of my adult years those verses were like books on the shelf that I had read at one time or another. And that's just where those verses stayed most of the time—on the shelves of my mind. There, these could be referenced in hard times, kind of like taking medicine for when I was sick. It never occurred to me that this thinking was another one of the devil's tricks. I had no idea that I could daily live in confidence and joy by meditating on these Bible verses. But now I know!

You can break the power of negative thoughts and feelings, and it's super easy to do! Meditate—think it over and over in your mind—on God's Word! I even write Bible verses out on notecards and keep them close by. You might be thinking this seems a bit extreme, but extreme circumstances require extreme action! When it comes to daily living in this world, I think we'd agree that extreme circumstances happen!

A PERSONAL ADMISSION

Anxiety is a battleground for me personally, and I can tell whether I'm winning or losing the daily battle. You'd think that since I'm the one writing this book, I'd be winning this battle every day. The truth is that some days I bound out of bed without a thought of needing God's Word, and several days like this will string together. It isn't too many days, however, that I'm waylaid by the enemy and I go running to God's Word. (Just a confession: running to God's Word wasn't always my first option—it was usually relying on my own instincts. That never worked out too well, so a word to my wise readers—be quick to run to God's Word.)

Sometimes I feel insecure around people who seem sure about themselves, have achieved higher goals than me, seem better polished or display better self-control, or are better educated. If I let those insecure feelings take the reins, I'll for sure say or do something dumb, then beat myself up for it for the next twenty-four hours. When my feelings of insecurities start, I now confront them with 2 Corinthians 5:21 and tell myself that I'm the righteousness of God in Christ Jesus. To me, this means that I'm accepted by God because of Christ's sacrifice, and His thoughts about me are all that really matter.

Sometimes I get anxious about things that could happen personally or things happening in the world around me. My verse to meditate on is John 10:10: "The thief's purpose is to steal and kill and destroy. My purpose is to give them a rich and satisfying life." Then receive this promise by thanking Jesus for a rich (like peace of mind) and satisfying life. When trials come (and they come to all of us), I think on Romans 8:28: "God causes everything to work together for the good of those who love God." A favorite of my dad's and now mine is Psalm 23:6: "Surely your goodness and unfailing love will pursue me all the days of my life, and I will live in the house of the LORD forever." If you stop to think about it, that's a win-win, on earth and heaven!

When you're feeling like you don't matter, meditate on Psalm 139:14 (NIV): "I praise you because I am fearfully and wonderfully made" and 1 John 3:1: "See how very much our Father loves us, for he calls us his children, and that is what we are!" Remembering how much God loves me really gives me self-worth.

Additionally, this verse will really lift you: "God loved us and chose us in Christ to be holy and without fault in his eyes" (Ephesians 1:4). What a comfort to know that I'm without fault in God's eyes when I've really messed things up!

Having trouble, problems, or fear? There are dozens of Bible verses that promise God will deliver us out of them. Psalm 62:8 (NIV) tells us to "trust in him at all times, you people; pour out your hearts to him, for God is our refuge." And Psalm 46:1 says, "God is our refuge and strength, always ready to help in times of trouble." One of my quick go-to verses is in Psalm 56:3 (NKJV): "Whenever I am afraid, I will trust in You." This verse, too, is a source of calmness: "For God has not given us a spirit of fear and timidity, but of power, love, and self-discipline" (2 Timothy 1:7). I've known these Bible verses most of my life but never thought to actually "eat" them. By that I mean apply it personally in my mind. God wrote these promises just for me! He wrote these promises just for you, too!

Wow, this is just a little scratch on the surface of digging into God's promises found in His Word, the Bible! It's the only offensive piece to what's known as the Armor of God: "And take the sword of the Spirit, which is the word of God" (Ephesians 6:17). Use it

ROUGH WATERS AHEAD

and you are wielding a mighty spiritual weapon!

WRAP-UP

As this is our final wrap-up, take a moment to peruse the chapter titles or wrap-ups. Did one of them stand out to you? Take the time to reread it because most likely that's an area that you might need some more encouragement. Drill down into God's Word because there is a whole lot more! There are many resources that have done the hard work for you by lining up Bible verses by subject areas. One resource specifically for teens that has done this is *The Secret Power of God's Word for Teens*, by Joyce Meyer. Happy digging!

YOUR EPIDERMIS IS SHOWING

REFLECT AND WRITE

Is there one Bible verse that you'd really like to memorize and hide in your heart? Write it here, then write it somewhere else where you will see it often.

_____
_____
_____
_____
_____
_____
_____
_____
_____
_____
_____
_____
_____

ROUGH WATERS AHEAD

AN AFTERWORD ABOUT YOUR SOUL

In our first chapter, we talked about the origin of drama. Do you remember what happened? Adam and Eve made a choice to disobey their Creator, God. Sin came into the world and the evidence is all around us. God could have thrown up His hands and left the rest of mankind to suffer the consequences. But He didn't! That's because God is love, holy, and just. Because of this, He sent and allowed His only Son, Jesus Christ, to take the punishment for our sin. "For I was born a sinner—yes, from the moment my mother conceived me" (Psalm 51:5). "For everyone has sinned; we all fall short of God's glorious standard" (Romans 3:23). All you have to do is accept God's love and forgiveness for your sin.

Why don't you make that choice now? Just pray, "Lord Jesus, I know that I have sinned. I believe you are the Son of God and that you died for my sins and rose again. I ask you to forgive me of all my sins. I ask you to come into my life to be my Savior and Lord. Thank you, Lord Jesus, for saving me. In Jesus' name, amen."

ROUGH WATERS AHEAD

So what's next? First, you should know that if you prayed the above prayer, the angels in heaven are having a party! Now, find a Bible and begin to read it. The books of Psalms or John are a good place to start. Also, find a group of teens who follow Christ and join in.

ABOUT THE AUTHOR

Faith Seiglie is a retired North Carolina public school teacher and currently resides with her husband near Emerald Isle, North Carolina. She has taught in both Christian and public schools. She began her career in the elementary grades before joining the ranks of middle school teachers. Her pivot to middle school came after one particular year when the stomach bug persisted among her first-grade students for almost the entire school year. After being "erupted on" one last time just weeks before summer break, she made the decision to move to a grade where students were mature enough to get to the trash can! The very next school year, she was teaching middle school language arts and soon realized this age group was her heart's desire! God can use anything, even projectile body fluid, to get us onto the path we're meant to walk!

Over the years, Faith has served on various school committees and was once named Teacher of the Year by her colleagues. She has served as Children's Church Director and Sunday School teacher. She and her husband currently serve on the mission board, Hearts for Heaven, which they have done for over a decade.

She is currently part of the praise and worship team at her church, Chapel by the Sea. Writing this book was something God put on her heart after seeing so many Christian and non-Christian kids alike struggle to navigate the tempestuous middle school years.